MY ALPHABET

By
E. K. Davis

Illustrated by Pat Stewart

GOLDEN PRESS ● NEW YORK
Western Publishing Company, Inc., Racine, Wisconsin

Library of Congress Catalog Card Number: 80-85086   ISBN 0-307-10104-5 / ISBN 0-307-68104-1 (lib. bdg.)
B C D E F G H I J

A is for apple,
Red and bright.

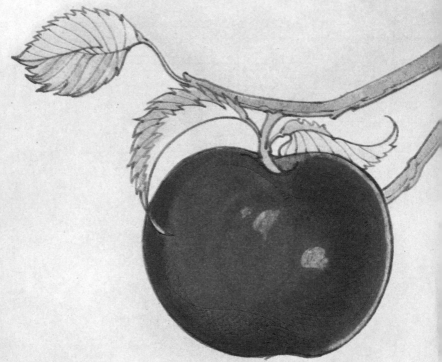

B is for bed,
Where I sleep at night.

C is for carrot,
Crunchy and yummy.

D is for dog.
He lies on his tummy.

E is for elephant.
She likes a shower.

F is for flag.
It flies from a tower.

G is for grapes.
They grow in a bunch.

H is for hamster.
She's eating her lunch.

I is for ice cream,
Cold and sweet.

J

is for jelly.
What a nice treat!

grape jelly

K is for kitten,
Playing with yarn.

L is for lamb.
He lives in the barn.

M is for mirror.
I see my face!

N is for nest,
In a high place.

O is for owl,
Flying at night.

P is for pear.
Have a big bite!

Q is for quilt,
All cozy and warm.

R is for rainbow,
After a storm.

S is for sun.
It shines in the sky.

T is for telephone.
Say "Hello!" and
"Good-by!"

U is for umbrella.
The rain won't come through.

V is for valentine.
It says "I love you."

W is for watch.
Listen, it ticks!

X is for xylophone.
Make music with sticks.

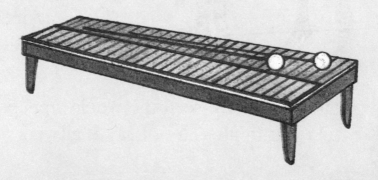

Y is for yo-yo.
It goes down, then
comes back.

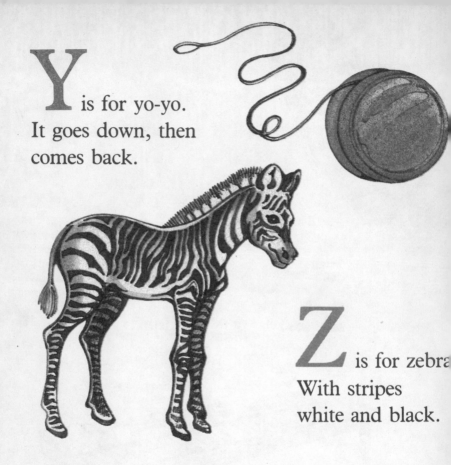

Z is for zebra
With stripes
white and black.

Now you have seen the whole alphabet.
Do you think you can say it all yet?